Tikkun Klali

Tikkun Klali

Rebbe Nahman of Bratzlav's
Ten Remedies for the Soul

Translated by
Rabbi Zalman Schachter-Shalomi

Foreword by
Netanel Miles-Yépez

Albion
Andalus

Boulder, Colorado
2013

*"The old shall be renewed,
and the new shall be made holy."*
— Rabbi Avraham Yitzhak Kook

Albion-Andalus Inc.
P. O. Box 19852
Boulder, CO 80308
www.albionandalus.com

Text design and composition by Albion-Andalus Inc.

Cover artwork by Rebekah Sipos.

Graphic design by Sari Wisenthal-Shore.

Manufactured in the United States of America

ISBN-13: 978-0615758763 (Albion-Andalus Books)
ISBN-10: 0615758762

ACKNOWLEDGMENTS

I wish to thank my student, Netanel Miles-Yépez, for editing my translation of the psalms, and for providing the Foreword; Rebekah Sipos for making the cover artwork, and Leigh Ann Dillinger for reading over the manuscript.

— Z.M.S-S.

PREFACE

THE GREAT HASIDIC MASTER, Rabbi Nahman of Bratzlav truly understood what it is to live with the body and the soul and between them. While in his youth he had gone through an ascetic period—sometimes swallowing his food without chewing it, so as to bypass his taste buds—he later spoke very respectfully and amazingly of how one has to have compassion on the body and "teach it everything that the soul knows." Looking at the way in which earlier kabbalists, who were firmly committed to asceticism, had created numerous tariffs of fast days for a variety of sins—some intentional, some unintentional, and some simply brought on by life—Reb Nahman, in compassion, sought for and found another way to expiate such sins through the recitation of these ten Psalms.

The deep reasons for Rebbe Nahman's choice of these ten particular Psalms is still a mystery to me. That they relate to the "ten kinds of arrows," the "ten kinds of poisons," and the "ten kinds of pulses" mentioned in his *Tale of the Seven Beggars* is clear; but *How?* and *Why?* are still a mystery for me. Nevertheless, I believe that he saw this 'decade' and association of various tens extending from the origin of the universe as fractals all the way down to our world, and had a special insight into them, and did himself understand *How?* and *Why?* they worked.

Therefore, I and many others have found that reciting these ten psalms, especially at his gravesite in Uman, but also anywhere and at any time, creates a release from the burden of guilt that can obscure a person's path to and reconciliation with a loving God. So I am delighted to follow the promptings of my student, Reb Netanel Miles-Yépez, to see these in print, in my own translation, and to further the reach of Rebbe Nahman's *tikkun ha'klali*, his 'general remedy.'

Rabbi Zalman Schachter-Shalomi

November 7th (22 Mar-Heshvan) 2012, the day we celebrated the good news.

FOREWORD

REBBE NAHMAN OF BRATZLAV (1772-1810), the great-grandson of Hasidism's founder, the holy Ba'al Shem Tov, is unquestionably one of the most original and significant personalities in the whole history of Hasidism. Even now, over 200 years after his death, interest in his life and teachings have only grown. In many ways, he is still a living presence in Hasidism, especially for Bratzlaver Hasidim, who continue to look to him as their *rebbe*, as a shepherd from the other side of life who guides them through his teachings and counsels, and who advocates for them with God each day as they pray.

Why should they believe this? Because Rebbe Nahman had himself left them with assurances before his death, promising to remain available to them in the next world. Shortly after he began to show symptoms of the tuberculosis that would eventually take his life, he began to speak for the first time of his desire for Hasidim to visit his grave after his death. Far from thinking morbidly of the prospect, he spoke constantly of how much pleasure these visits would afford him, and how he wished each visitor to recite psalms at his grave—ten particular psalms he called a *tikkun klali*, a 'general remedy':[1]

> When my days are over and I leave this world, I will intercede for anyone who comes to my grave, says these ten psalms and gives a [coin] to charity. No matter how great his sins, I will do everything in my

---

1 Nathan of Breslov, trans. Avraham Greenbaum, *Tzaddik: A Portrait of Rabbi Nachman*, 68-70.

power, spanning the length and breadth of creation, to cleanse and protect him. . . . I will pull him out of *Gehennom* by his *peyos!* It makes no difference who it may be or how seriously he may have sinned. All he has to do is to take upon himself not to return to his folly.[2]

For this reason, thousands upon thousands of pilgrims visit the grave of Rebbe Nahman in Uman, Ukraine, every year, hoping that he will intercede from them. They travel to his gravesite, give a little charity, and pray the *tikkun klali*, the 'general remedy.'

A general remedy for what? In earlier centuries, schools of kabbalists had instituted a host of penances for expiating guilt for various kinds of sins. These penances, though often quite extreme, were nevertheless seized upon with eagerness by the generations of kabbalists that followed, for they offered a *means* of relief, a *way* to get clean again. They included fairly severe prescriptions for afflicting the offending flesh—considered the source of most sins—such as dipping in freezing water and fasting specific numbers of days for each offence.

Often, the "sins" which most concerned these male kabbalists had to do with sex and the "wasting" of seminal fluid, almost certainly because the sex drive so persistently and successfully pushes its own agenda, usually running contrary to and foiling the spiritual practitioner's most carefully laid plans. Having failed to subdue these urges—despite the best of intentions and the most sincere efforts—these serious seekers of God often found themselves bereft and burdened with a guilt for which they desperately wished to be forgiven.

---

2 Chaim Kramer, *Through Fire and Water*, 172-73. See also Nathan of Breslov, *Tzaddik*, 123.

Today, as then, we struggle with the same basic issues, trying to live a deeply *human* life, a deeply *spiritual* life, while still being subjected to our most basic animal desires and instincts. A knowledge of psychology has given us some explanation for our behaviors, and thus some freedom from certain kinds of guilt; but we are still tormented by our persistent failures and inadequacies, again and again, watching our most noble ambitions and good intentions fall to intense and immediate desires. And having, once again, 'messed up,' we ask ourselves, "How will I ever bridge the gap?" Having gotten lost again, we ask, "What road will take us home? What is the *means* of return?"

In answer, the kabbalists of the past offered extremely heavy and exacting penances to expiate particular sins; but Rebbe Nahman took pity on us and searched for a less burdensome 'general remedy' to cover all such sins. I say, "searched," because he did not take this task lightly. You see, the old penances were not *merely* self-flagellating attempts to subdue the flesh. They were often intricately tied to sacred teachings from the kabbalistic tradition that made them, at least in the eyes of those who used them, spiritually effective for cleansing the soul. Thus, Rebbe Nahman could not simply dismiss them. He had to find a new 'technology' to accomplish the same end, and one that would cover the entire spectrum of sins, as his great disciple, Reb Nosson of Nemirov, explains:

Now, it is an extremely onerous task indeed for a person to [remedy] each of his sins individually, since they are so very numerous. In fact, it is impossible to [remedy] them, insofar as each Torah prohibition contains many fine points and details [and a person cannot possibly identify and correct all of them]. Therefore, one must effect an overall, [general remedy] *(Tikkun HaKlali)* for all of these sins [. . .] Through this, all the Torah prohibitions that a person transgressed are [remedied] automatically. Even the narrowest and most slender places which no [other] [remedy] can reach can be corrected by the [general remedy], which directs rectification to those places as well.[3]

That is to say, Rebbe Nahman had discovered a universal key to open any lock, a spiritual antidote to counteract any poison, ten psalms which, when recited together, address the negative effects of any kind of sin. These ten psalms are: 16, 32, 41, 42, 59, 77, 90, 105, 137, and 150.

Why ten psalms? And why these ten in particular? It is difficult to say. In Rebbe Nahman's famous *Tale of the Seven Beggars*, on the sixth day, we hear about the "ten kinds of arrows," the "ten kinds of poison," the "ten kinds of wisdom," the "ten kinds of pulse," the "ten kinds of wind," and the "ten kinds of song."[4] The associations for these various tens are too many and too complex to elaborate here, but suffice it say that the ten arrows may refer to the ten kinds of spiritual damage caused by different sins, and the ten songs to the healing powers of the psalms, which are themselves songs.[5]

Now, Rebbe Nahman teaches that any ten psalms together contain the ten kinds of song, but the ten that comprise the *tikkun klali* are the most powerful combination. Why? We do not know. Rebbe Nahman did not tell us why he chose these ten psalms in particular. Nevertheless, it is enough for many to know that he recommended them.

3 Noson of Nemirov, trans. Yaakov Gabel, *Abridged Likutey Moharan*, Vol. 1, 265.
4 See Nahman of Bratzlav, trans. Zalman Schachter-Shalomi, *Tale of the Seven Beggars*, 49-55.
5 See Nachman of Breslov, trans. Aryeh Kaplan, *Rabbi Nachman's Stories*, notes pages 411-15, 418-20.

In most Bratzlaver synagogues, the *tikkun klali* is recited regularly on *Shabbat* morning, after *mussaf*, though some Bratzlaver Hasidim also recite it every day. Rabbi Tzvi Aryeh Rosenfeld, one of the great Bratzlaver leaders of the 20th century, instituted the custom among his students of reciting the *tikkun klali* each day after their prayers.[6] But the *tikkun klali* may be recited anywhere, at any time there is a need, whenever one's relationship with God feels out of balance. If possible, the person reciting the *tikkun klali* might dip in a *mikveh* beforehand, and afterward, offer some charity. What is most important is that they reach out in sincere repentance with each psalm, and commit themselves to a life that is in accord with that repentance, remembering what Rebbe Nahman says, "You must not despair! Never give up!"

Netanel Miles-Yépez
Boulder, Colorado 2013

---

6 Chaim Kramer, *Crossing the Narrow Bridge*, 132.

* TIKKUN *
I

Psalm 16
(David's imprinted song.)

God!
Keep me safe,
For I have taken
Cover in You.

I have said to *Yah*—
You are my Sustainer;
Although I am
Of little worth,
You are good
And kind to me.

But not so the idols!
The earthbound
Think of the idols
As sacred and mighty,

1

Supposing their desires
Will be fulfilled by them.

Rushing after idols,
Their sorrows will increase!
I will not make libations
Of blood to them;
I will not put their names
Upon my lips!

Yah! You are
My chosen portion
And my own cup;
You keep me in Your care;
Your Providence
Is pleasing to me;
What a good heritage
Is mine now.

I will bless *Yah!*
For Your counsels,
The wise guidance
You give me in dreams;
I place myself constantly
In Your Presence;
I will not falter
Because You
Are at my side.

Therefore,
My heart is joyous,
My innards feel delight,
My body is serene;
For You will not
Abandon my soul
To torment,
Neither will You
Let Your devotee
Be disappointed.

Please!
Make me know
The path of life;
The fulfillment of happiness
Is in Your presence;
May I forever
Feel the pleasures
Of Your kindness.

* TIKKUN *
II

Psalm 32
(David's 'get smart' song.)

Blissful and glad
Is one who
Experiences forgiveness,
The remission of sins.

Blissful and glad
Is the one
Whose worst sin is
To be at times
Unmindful of God,
And who does not
Fool oneself.

I suffered in silence,
My bones withered
As I wept all day long.

You, yes You,
Did weigh me down
Day and night,
Turning my vital fluids
Into parched clods—
Selah!

I told You
Of my sin;
I did not hide
My wrongdoing.
I said it:
I will confess
That I rebelled
Against You, *Yah,*
And You lifted
My warped failings
From me—
Selah!

For this,
Whenever one
Finds a moment,
Let all the devout
Pray to You,
So that they
Will not be
Overwhelmed

Or burned-out.
You are my refuge,
Protecting me
From adversity,
A song of deliverance,
Shielding me.

(God responds:)
Let me help you,
Give you wisdom,
Show you a way to go,
Enlighten you a bit,
Steer you and keep an eye on you;
Don't be like a horse, a mule,
Heedless of the rein and bit
That urges them to stop;
Don't let this happen to you.

Many are the aches
Of the depraved—
But one who is
Secured in *Yah*
Is surrounded
By kindness.

Take joy in *Yah*,
Tzaddikim,
Righteous Ones,

Keep singing,
Revel in God's light
All you who are
Sincere of heart.

* TIKKUN *
III

Psalm 41

(David's song to succeed in overcoming.)

Blissful and glad
Is one who cares
For the poor.

On a bad day, *Yah*
Will give her refuge;
Yah will protect
And invigorate him,
Make her happy
Right here on earth,
And not hand him over
To the malice of her foes.

On the sick bed,
Yah will support him;

8

Yah will bed her down
In comfort.

I always said:
'*Yah,* be kind,
Heal my spirit—
Though I failed You.'

My foes say that
I am in a bad place,
Soon to die,
To be forgotten,
Spying on me
And then telling lies;
In their hearts,
They gather clues
To spread rumors;
My enemies become a gang
Grumbling about me,
Plotting my downfall;
Low-lives, scheming
To poison me,
Hoping that once
I'm flat on my back,
I won't ever get up again;
Even one of my friends,
Who broke bread with me—
O how I trusted him—

Turned on his heels
And abandoned me!

But You, *Yah,*
Be kind and help me up,
So I can make them peaceful!

In this, will I know
That you like me—
If my opponent
Will not be punished
On my account.

I will rely on
Guileless ways,
So I can stand
Forever free
Before You.

Blessed are You,
Yah, Israel's God,
From world to world—
Amen, yes, Amen!

* TIKKUN *
IV

Psalm 42

(A Korahite song to succeed in overcoming.)

Like a gazelle
Yearning, thirsting
For water,
So too my soul,
She longs,
My God,
For You.

My soul thirsts
For You, God,
The Living God;
When, when will I
Get to see
My God's face?

My tears
Were my bread
Day and night;
My oppressors
Taunted me
Constantly—
(Your temple is destroyed!)
"So where is your God?"

I pour out my soul—
What memories!
I would proudly pace
In my pilgrimage
To God's house,
Parading with songs
Of festive appreciation.

Why be upset
My spirit?
Why be so upset?
Put your hope in God—
Yes, I will thank Him again
For having faced me
With Her help.

My God,
In my depths,
I bow to You;

Distant from Jordan's land,
Far from Hermon's highlands,
I try to picture them again.

Deep calls unto deep.
Breakers, waves, surf
Overtake me;
By day, I feel
How You deploy
Your kindness;
By night, You sing
With me a prayer
To the living God.

I say to You,
My God, my fortress—
Why did You forget me?
Why should I dart around,
Dreading the oppression
Of the enemy?

There is terror
In my bones,
Sneers of ridicule
From my foes;
All day long
They taunt me:
"Where is your God?"

Why be upset
My spirit?
Why be so upset?
Put your hope in God—
Yes, I will thank Him again
For having faced me
With Her help.

Judge me God
And fight my battle
Against people who
Know not kindness;
Save me—
From a cheat,
An abuser;
You Who are
The God,
My stronghold—
Why did You
Leave me behind?
Why should I have
To keep dodging about,
Dreading the cruelty
Of the enemy?

Send Your light
And Your truth!
Let these be my guides

And bring me safely
To Your Holy mountain,
To the sacred place
Where You are
Present.

I will approach
God's altar,
The God who is
Our God,
The source of
My bliss;
My God,
I will thank You,
And with my guitar,
Sing to You.

Why be upset
My spirit?
Why be so upset?
Put your hope in God—
Yes, I will thank Him again
For having faced me
With Her help.

* TIKKUN *
V

Psalm 59

(To overcome and not be destroyed. David's song when Saul sent assassins and they surrounded the house.)

Save me, my God,
From my enemies,
Those who rear
Themselves over me;
Raise me up above them;
Release me from
Those who work evil;
Save me from
Those who thirst
For blood;
They lie in wait
To kill me;
These muggers
Slink after me,

And I, *Yah,*
Have not rebelled
Or failed.

And You, *Yah,*
God of Hosts,
God of Israel,
Rear up over
These thugs;
Don't be kind to
Traitors and sinners—
Selah!

At sunset,
They'll come back,
Howling like dogs;
They will surge
Through the town,
Bellowing with
Their maws,
Their mouths
Cutting like swords;
They act as if
No one gives
A damn;
And You, *Yah,*
Ridicule them,
Mocking the felons.

I am alert
For Your power,
Because You
Lift me up;
My God—
Let Your kindness
Reach me soon!
God will see
To my triumph!

Don't kill them, God;
People might forget—
But with Your power
Remove them
And bring them down
For all to see and learn,
Our Sustainer,
Our shield.

Their mouths sin
When they speak;
They are tripped up
By their pride;
They tell tales,
Cursing and lying;
Consume them
With Your wrath;
Consume them

Until they are gone;
Make them know
That there is a God,
Supreme in Jacob
And extending to
The ends of the earth—
Selah!

At sunset,
They'll come back,
Howling like dogs;
They'll drift
Through the town,
Ravenous and vagrant.

You have been
My upholder,
My Refuge,
When I was hunted;
My strong One,
I will sing to You;
God, you are
My uplift,
My kind
God.

* TIKKUN *
VI

Psalm 77

*(An overcoming song by Assaf to be accompanied by
a sweet sounding instrument.)*

I raise
My voice
To cry out
To You, God!
I raised
My voice
And You gave
Ear to me;
When I was
Attacked,
My Sustainer,
I sought You;
I strained
Toward You,
Inconsolable;

Then I remembered
To sing to You
At night,
My searching
Spirit talks
With You
In my heart.

(I asked myself:)
Will my Sustainer
Abandon me forever?
Will He not relent?
Has all Her kindness
Been all used up?
Has He stopped
Communicating
With our generation?
I remember God
And I sigh;
I speak up
And my spirit
Gets faint,
Selah!

You kept me
From falling
Asleep
While my heart

Beat wildly;
I could not speak;
I gave thought
To earlier days,
Years of worlds
Long gone;
Did God ever forget
To be gracious?
Did His anger
Squash Her mercy?!
Selah!

So I mused—
My prayer reaches—
The Most High
Will help again;
Let me recall
The works of *Yah*;
I do remember
Your wonders
Of the past;
So I reflect
On all Your actions
And I talk about
The unfolding
Of Your involved
Scenarios.

God,
Your way
Is in holiness;
Is there a God
As great as You, God?
You are the God
Who performs miracles;
Even the nations know
Of Your power;
With a strong arm
You redeemed
Your people,
Descendants of
Jacob and Joseph—
Selah!

The glaciers
Have seen You;
They saw You
And trembled;
So too did
The deeps
Rumble
And quake;
The clouds rained
In torrents;
The skies replied
With thunder;

23

The tempest
Broke through
With a crash;
The whirlwinds
You made
Thundered forth;
Lightning bolts
Flashed in space;
Earth rumbled
And quaked;
You make a way
Even in the sea;
You set paths
In mighty waters;
Where You set foot
Is a mystery to us.

Through all
These upheavals,
You lead Your flock,
Your people,
At the hands of
Moses and Aaron.

* TIKKUN *
VII

Psalm 90

(Moses, God's man at prayer.)

Master!
You are
Our home
Each time
We are
Born again.

Before
Mountains
Emerged,
Before Earth
And Space
Were born,
From Cosmos
To Cosmos,
You are God.

You bring us,
Poor and weak
To death's door
And You urge us:
"Return, Adam's kin!"

In Your gaze,
A millennium is as
Yesterday gone,
Like a watch at night.

You flooded us
With sleep;
Morning had us
As wilted hay.

Blossoming
With dawn,
Only to change
At dusk,
All wilted
And dry.

Your wrath
Makes us panic;
Your anger
Confuses us.

All our
Crooked places
Are open
To Your gaze;
Our hidden
Stirrings,
Are visible
To Your
Inner light.

We note
All our days,
Fleeing from
Your ire;
Our years
Are fading
Like a fleeting
Thought.

Our lifespan's days
Are seventy years,
And if hardy,
Eighty years;
Their gain
Is struggle
And offense;
Soon we are
Chopped down,

Dispersed
And gone;
Who can
Estimate
The extent
Of Your rage?
Fear of Your ire
Paralyzes us.

Make us
Aware enough
To treasure
Our days;
A wise heart
Brings vision.

How long
It seems—
Relent!
I am in
Your service;
Become
Reconciled
With me.

Gladden us,
No less than You
Made us suffer—

Those years we
Endured such harm.

Oh that
We could see
Your design clearly,
Your grandeur
In our children.

May Your
Kindly Presence,
Our Sustainer,
Be pleasant
For us ever;
May our
Hands' efforts
Achieve their aim;
Please, let our efforts
Result in good!

* TIKKUN *
VIII

Psalm 105

Thank God—
His fame is
Our watchword;
Make Her deeds known
Among the peoples;
Sing and make
Music to Him:
Talk of all Her
Wondrous works;
Glory in His
Holy name:
Let the heart
Of those
Who search
For *Yah*, rejoice;
Seek *Yah*,

And Her power,
When His strength
Is what You need;
But place Yourself
In Her Presence
All the time;
Remember that
He has done
Marvelous things;
Her wonders
Are amazing;
And how fair
His judgments are
O seed of Abraham,
Her servant!
You children of Jacob,
His chosen ones!
She is *Yah*, our God:
His judgments are
Of global importance.

She constantly
Remembered
His covenant,
The commandments
Which She declared—
For a thousand
Generations;

Which covenant
He made with Abraham,
And Her oath to Isaac;
And confirmed the same
As law to Jacob and Israel
For an everlasting covenant:
Saying—Unto You will I
Give the land of Canaan,
The lot of Your inheritance:
When they were but
A few in number;
Very few, and
Strangers in that land.
Even though they
Wandered, displaced,
From one nation to another,
From one kingdom
To another people;
He permitted no one
To do them wrong;
For their sakes,
She took even kings to task;
Saying—Don't touch
My anointed ones!
Do no harm to my prophets.

Earlier, He had called
For a famine upon the land:

Every loaf of bread ruined;
Sending a person before them—
Joseph was sold to be a slave;
They hurt his foot with shackles:
His body was slapped in irons
Until the time when they
Did mention him to Pharaoh;
The decree of *Yah* purified him;
The king, a powerful ruler of peoples,
Unchained and freed him;
He appointed him
Manager of his domain,
Administrator of his realm,
Chief of his advisors,
And had him teach his elders wisdom.

Israel came into Egypt;
So it was that Jacob settled
In the land of Ham;
And *God* increased
Her People greatly;
And made them stronger
Than their oppressors;
He turned the Egyptians' heart
To hate Her people,
To plot against His servants;
She sent Moses, His servant,
And Aaron, whom She had chosen;

They (Moses and Aaron)
Placed words of His signs
Among the Egyptians,
Wonders in the land of Ham;
She sent darkness, and made it dark;
And they did not defy His word;
She turned their waters into blood,
He killed their fish;
Their land crawled with frogs,
Even in the chambers of their kings!
She spoke, and there came lots of beasts,
Lice in all their borders!
Instead of rain, He sent hail,
Flaming fire in their land!
She slashed their vines
And their fig trees;
He shattered the trees of their borders;
She decreed, and the locusts came,
Grasshoppers without number,
And ate up the green in their land,
Devoured the fruit of their ground;
He killed all the firstborn in their land,
The first of all their potency;
She liberated them,
Enriching them with silver and gold;
Not one of them was feeble,
Not one among their tribes was frail;

Egypt was happy when they departed,
For the fear of the Israelites befell them.

He spread a cloud for a screen,
And fire to give light in the night;
Israel asked and She brought on quail,
And the bread of heaven
Satisfied them;
He opened the rock,
And the waters gushed forth,
And in the desert
They flowed like a river.

For She remembered
Abraham, His servant,
And kept Her sacred pledge;
He brought forth Her people with joy,
His chosen folk with joyous song;
He gave them the lands of the heathen;
They inherited all for which
The pagans had worked;
All so that they would
Keep Her statutes,
And follow His guidance—
Halleluyah!

* TIKKUN *
IX

Psalm 137

We sat
By the rivers of Babylon,
We remembered Zion
And wept from grief.

Our captors asked of us:
Sing for us of the songs of Zion!
We like the words of Your song;
Accompany them with
Your instruments!

But we hid our harps
Among the willows:
How can we sing
The song of our Sustainer,
In a foreign land?

Forgetting You,
Jerusalem,
Is like losing the
Use of my hands!
I'd rather lose
My voice and speech
Than forget Jerusalem!

O Jerusalem!
I have no happiness
Away from You!

Yah! —
Do not forget the day
Our enemies demolished
The foundations of Your House;
Villains of Babylon!
You smashed the
Skulls of our babies
Against the rocks!
I feel such grief and rage
That I want to bless anyone
Who would do to You
What You did to us!

* TIKKUN *
X

Psalm 150

Halleluyah!
Praise God!
In His sanctuary;
Praise Him powerfully
To the sky.

Praise Her for
Her potent acts;
Praise Her for
Her Generosity.

Praise Him
With trumpet sound;
Praise Him
With strings and harp.

Praise Her
With drum and dance;
Praise Her
With organ and flute.

Praise Him
With crashing cymbals;
Praise Him
With resonant cymbals;
Let all souls praise *Yah*—
Halleluyah!

At this point, Bratzlaver Hasidim praying the *tikkun klali* usually recite a prayer composed by Reb Nosson of Nemirov; but since Rebbe Nahman and Reb Nosson taught that people should also pray the words that come from within, I suggest you take a moment now to pray from the heart around the issue that has caused you to recite the *tikkun klali* today.

— Z.M.S-S.

* Appendix *

For those who have trouble reciting Psalm 137 because of its difficult content (which must be understood in its proper context), Psalm 139 might be seen as a good alternative. However, in suggesting this, I am in no way making a claim that it is an efficacious substitute for Psalm 137 with regard to the practice of the *tikkun klali*.

— Z.M.S-S.

Psalm 139

(Conductor — David's prayer set to music.)

Yah!
You have scanned
And discerned me;
You know when
I am relaxed
Or agitated;
From afar,
You comprehend
My fantasies.
You design

My conduct
And my repose;
You direct
My paths
So I can
Manage.

Before
My mouth
Opens,
You know
What I am
About to say;
You have
Shaped my past
And my future;
Your hand,
Gently on my
Shoulder.

All this
Awes my
Awareness;
It is beyond
My skills
To fathom.

Where to
Can I withdraw
From Your spirit?
Flee from
Facing You?

If I would
Mount up
To Heaven,
There You are!
If I make
My bed in Hell,
You are there too!

Soaring on the
Wings of the Dawn,
To find shelter
In the setting Sun,
It would be Your hand,
That would carry me,
Your right hand,
Holding me safe!

If I want to
Find oblivion
In night-shadow,
Trading light
For darkness,

To You, it would
Still not be dark;
Night is as bright
As day for You;
Dark and light—
The same in
Your sight.

You have designed
My innards, shaped me
In my mother's womb.

I am overcome
With gratitude
At Your awesome
Wonders,
Your astonishing
Works,
Of which my soul
Is aware.

My essence
Is not hidden
From You,
Who have made me
In concealment,
Who has knitted me
Beneath the surface.

Your eyes
Have seen me
As an embryo;
My days are
All inscribed
In Your ledger—
Days not yet shaped—
Each one of them
Counted.

How precious
Are Your stirrings
In me, God!
How powerful
Their impact!
I can't number them—
Beyond the grains of sand!
When I emerge
From my reflection,
I am still with You.

If You, God,
Would only rid us
From our evil!
If only the cruelty
Would disappear!
And defiance
Of You vanish,

Forgiveness
Overtaking
Enmity!

I detest hatred
Of You, *Yah!*
Quarrelsomeness
Repels me;
I loathe hostility
To the utmost.

God! I open myself
To Your scrutiny;
Know what is
In my heart;
Examine and know
My longings;
See and remove
Any defiance
From me,
And guide me
In the way
That serves
Your intent
For our Earth.

* Appendix *

For those who have trouble reciting Psalm 137 because of its difficult content (which must be understood in its proper context), Psalm 139 might be seen as a good alternative. However, in suggesting this, I am in no way making a claim that it is an efficacious substitute for Psalm 137 with regard to the practice of the *tikkun klali*.

פרק קלט

א לַמְנַצֵּחַ לְדָוִד מִזְמוֹר יְהוָה חֲקַרְתַּנִי וַתֵּדָע: ב אַתָּה יָדַעְתָּ
שִׁבְתִּי וְקוּמִי בַּנְתָּה לְרֵעִי מֵרָחוֹק: ג אָרְחִי וְרִבְעִי זֵרִיתָ
וְכָל־דְּרָכַי הִסְכַּנְתָּה: ד כִּי אֵין מִלָּה בִּלְשׁוֹנִי הֵן יְהֹוָה יָדַעְתָּ
כֻלָּהּ: ה אָחוֹר וָקֶדֶם צַרְתָּנִי וַתָּשֶׁת עָלַי כַּפֶּכָה: ו פְּלָאֶיה
[פְּלִיאָה] דַעַת מִמֶּנִּי נִשְׂגְּבָה לֹא־אוּכַל לָהּ: ז אָנָה אֵלֵךְ
מֵרוּחֶךָ וְאָנָה מִפָּנֶיךָ אֶבְרָח: ח אִם־אֶסַּק שָׁמַיִם שָׁם אָתָּה
וְאַצִּיעָה שְּׁאוֹל הִנֶּךָּ: ט אֶשָּׂא כַנְפֵי־שָׁחַר אֶשְׁכְּנָה בְּאַחֲרִית
יָם: י גַּם־שָׁם יָדְךָ תַנְחֵנִי וְתֹאחֲזֵנִי יְמִינֶךָ: יא וָאֹמַר אַךְ־חֹשֶׁךְ
יְשׁוּפֵנִי וְלַיְלָה אוֹר בַּעֲדֵנִי: יב גַּם־חֹשֶׁךְ לֹא־יַחְשִׁיךְ מִמֶּךָ
וְלַיְלָה כַּיּוֹם יָאִיר כַּחֲשֵׁיכָה כָּאוֹרָה: יג כִּי־אַתָּה קָנִיתָ כִלְיֹתָי
תְּסֻכֵּנִי בְּבֶטֶן אִמִּי: יד אוֹדְךָ עַל כִּי נוֹרָאוֹת נִפְלֵיתִי נִפְלָאִים
מַעֲשֶׂיךָ וְנַפְשִׁי יֹדַעַת מְאֹד: טו לֹא־נִכְחַד עָצְמִי מִמֶּךָ
אֲשֶׁר־עֻשֵּׂיתִי בַסֵּתֶר רֻקַּמְתִּי בְּתַחְתִּיּוֹת אָרֶץ: טז גָּלְמִי | רָאוּ
עֵינֶיךָ וְעַל־סִפְרְךָ כֻּלָּם יִכָּתֵבוּ יָמִים יֻצָּרוּ וְלֹא [וְלוֹ] אֶחָד
בָּהֶם: יז וְלִי מַה־יָּקְרוּ רֵעֶיךָ אֵל מֶה עָצְמוּ רָאשֵׁיהֶם:
יח אֶסְפְּרֵם מֵחוֹל יִרְבּוּן הֱקִיצֹתִי וְעוֹדִי עִמָּךְ: יט אִם־תִּקְטֹל
אֱלוֹהַ | רָשָׁע וְאַנְשֵׁי דָמִים סוּרוּ מֶנִּי: כ אֲשֶׁר יֹאמְרֻךָ לִמְזִמָּה
נָשֻׂא לַשָּׁוְא עָרֶיךָ: כא הֲלוֹא־מְשַׂנְאֶיךָ יְהוָה | אֶשְׂנָא
וּבִתְקוֹמְמֶיךָ אֶתְקוֹטָט: כב תַּכְלִית שִׂנְאָה שְׂנֵאתִים לְאוֹיְבִים
הָיוּ לִי: כג חָקְרֵנִי אֵל וְדַע לְבָבִי בְּחָנֵנִי וְדַע שַׂרְעַפָּי: כד וּרְאֵה
אִם־דֶּרֶךְ־עֹצֶב בִּי וּנְחֵנִי בְּדֶרֶךְ עוֹלָם:)

* TIKKUN X *

פרק קנ

א הַלְלוּיָהּ | הַלְלוּ־אֵל בְּקָדְשׁוֹ הַלְלוּהוּ בִּרְקִיעַ עֻזּוֹ: ב הַלְלוּהוּ בִגְבוּרֹתָיו הַלְלוּהוּ כְּרֹב גֻּדְלוֹ: ג הַלְלוּהוּ בְּתֵקַע שׁוֹפָר הַלְלוּהוּ בְּנֵבֶל וְכִנּוֹר: ד הַלְלוּהוּ בְתֹף וּמָחוֹל הַלְלוּהוּ בְּמִנִּים וְעוּגָב: ה הַלְלוּהוּ בְצִלְצְלֵי־שָׁמַע הַלְלוּהוּ בְּצִלְצְלֵי תְרוּעָה: ו כֹּל הַנְּשָׁמָה תְּהַלֵּל יָהּ הַלְלוּיָהּ:

At this point, Bratzlaver Hasidim praying the *tikkun ha'klali* usually recite a prayer composed by Reb Nosson of Nemirov; but since Rebbe Nahman and Reb Nosson taught that people should also pray the words that come from within, I suggest you take a moment now to pray from the heart around the issue that has caused you to recite the *tikkun ha'klali*.

— Z.M.S-S.

* TIKKUN IX *

פרק קלז

א עַל־נַהֲרוֹת ׀ בָּבֶל שָׁם יָשַׁבְנוּ גַּם־בָּכִינוּ בְּזָכְרֵנוּ אֶת־צִיּוֹן׃
ב עַל־עֲרָבִים בְּתוֹכָהּ תָּלִינוּ כִּנֹּרוֹתֵינוּ׃ ג כִּי שָׁם שְׁאֵלוּנוּ
שׁוֹבֵינוּ דִּבְרֵי־שִׁיר וְתוֹלָלֵינוּ שִׂמְחָה שִׁירוּ לָנוּ מִשִּׁיר צִיּוֹן׃
ד אֵיךְ נָשִׁיר אֶת־שִׁיר יְהֹוָה עַל אַדְמַת נֵכָר׃ ה אִם־אֶשְׁכָּחֵךְ
יְרוּשָׁלִָם תִּשְׁכַּח יְמִינִי׃ ו תִּדְבַּק־לְשׁוֹנִי ׀ לְחִכִּי אִם־לֹא
אֶזְכְּרֵכִי אִם־לֹא אַעֲלֶה אֶת־יְרוּשָׁלִַם עַל רֹאשׁ שִׂמְחָתִי׃ ז זְכֹר
יְהֹוָה ׀ לִבְנֵי אֱדוֹם אֵת יוֹם יְרוּשָׁלִָם הָאֹמְרִים עָרוּ ׀ עָרוּ עַד
הַיְסוֹד בָּהּ׃ ח בַּת־בָּבֶל הַשְּׁדוּדָה אַשְׁרֵי שֶׁיְשַׁלֶּם־לָךְ
אֶת־גְּמוּלֵךְ שֶׁגָּמַלְתְּ לָנוּ׃ ט אַשְׁרֵי ׀ שֶׁיֹּאחֵז וְנִפֵּץ אֶת־עֹלָלַיִךְ
אֶל־הַסָּלַע׃

48

* TIKKUN VIII *

פרק קה

א הוֹדוּ לַיהוָה קִרְאוּ בִשְׁמוֹ הוֹדִיעוּ בָעַמִּים עֲלִילוֹתָיו: ב שִׁירוּ לוֹ
זַמְּרוּ־לוֹ שִׂיחוּ בְּכָל־נִפְלְאוֹתָיו: ג הִתְהַלְלוּ בְּשֵׁם קָדְשׁוֹ יִשְׂמַח לֵב |
מְבַקְשֵׁי יְהוָה: ד דִּרְשׁוּ יְהוָה וְעֻזּוֹ בַּקְּשׁוּ פָנָיו תָּמִיד: ה זִכְרוּ נִפְלְאוֹתָיו
אֲשֶׁר עָשָׂה מֹפְתָיו וּמִשְׁפְּטֵי־פִיו: ו זֶרַע אַבְרָהָם עַבְדּוֹ בְּנֵי יַעֲקֹב בְּחִירָיו:
ז הוּא יְהוָה אֱלֹהֵינוּ בְּכָל־הָאָרֶץ מִשְׁפָּטָיו: ח זָכַר לְעוֹלָם בְּרִיתוֹ דָּבָר
צִוָּה לְאֶלֶף דּוֹר: ט אֲשֶׁר כָּרַת אֶת־אַבְרָהָם וּשְׁבוּעָתוֹ לְיִשְׂחָק:
י וַיַּעֲמִידֶהָ לְיַעֲקֹב לְחֹק לְיִשְׂרָאֵל בְּרִית עוֹלָם: יא לֵאמֹר לְךָ אֶתֵּן
אֶת־אֶרֶץ כְּנָעַן חֶבֶל נַחֲלַתְכֶם: יב בִּהְיוֹתָם מְתֵי מִסְפָּר כִּמְעַט וְגָרִים
בָּהּ: יג וַיִּתְהַלְּכוּ מִגּוֹי אֶל־גּוֹי מִמַּמְלָכָה אֶל־עַם אַחֵר: יד לֹא־הִנִּיחַ אָדָם
לְעָשְׁקָם וַיּוֹכַח עֲלֵיהֶם מְלָכִים: טו אַל־תִּגְּעוּ בִמְשִׁיחָי וְלִנְבִיאַי
אַל־תָּרֵעוּ: טז וַיִּקְרָא רָעָב עַל־הָאָרֶץ כָּל־מַטֵּה־לֶחֶם שָׁבָר: יז שָׁלַח
לִפְנֵיהֶם אִישׁ לְעֶבֶד נִמְכַּר יוֹסֵף: יח עִנּוּ בַכֶּבֶל רַגְלָיו [רַגְלוֹ] בַּרְזֶל בָּאָה
נַפְשׁוֹ: יט עַד־עֵת בֹּא־דְבָרוֹ אִמְרַת יְהוָה צְרָפָתְהוּ: כ שָׁלַח מֶלֶךְ
וַיַּתִּירֵהוּ מֹשֵׁל עַמִּים וַיְפַתְּחֵהוּ: כא שָׂמוֹ אָדוֹן לְבֵיתוֹ וּמֹשֵׁל בְּכָל־קִנְיָנוֹ:
כב לֶאְסֹר שָׂרָיו בְּנַפְשׁוֹ וּזְקֵנָיו יְחַכֵּם: כג וַיָּבֹא יִשְׂרָאֵל מִצְרָיִם וְיַעֲקֹב גָּר
בְּאֶרֶץ־חָם: כד וַיֶּפֶר אֶת־עַמּוֹ מְאֹד וַיַּעֲצִמֵהוּ מִצָּרָיו: כה הָפַךְ לִבָּם
לִשְׂנֹא עַמּוֹ לְהִתְנַכֵּל בַּעֲבָדָיו: כו שָׁלַח מֹשֶׁה עַבְדּוֹ אַהֲרֹן אֲשֶׁר בָּחַר־בּוֹ:
כז שָׂמוּ־בָם דִּבְרֵי אֹתוֹתָיו וּמֹפְתִים בְּאֶרֶץ חָם: כח שָׁלַח חֹשֶׁךְ וַיַּחְשִׁךְ
וְלֹא־מָרוּ אֶת־דְּבָרָיו [דְּבָרוֹ]: כט הָפַךְ אֶת־מֵימֵיהֶם לְדָם וַיָּמֶת
אֶת־דְּגָתָם: ל שָׁרַץ אַרְצָם צְפַרְדְּעִים בְּחַדְרֵי מַלְכֵיהֶם: לא אָמַר וַיָּבֹא
עָרֹב כִּנִּים בְּכָל־גְּבוּלָם: לב נָתַן גִּשְׁמֵיהֶם בָּרָד אֵשׁ לֶהָבוֹת בְּאַרְצָם:
לג וַיַּךְ גַּפְנָם וּתְאֵנָתָם וַיְשַׁבֵּר עֵץ גְּבוּלָם: לד אָמַר וַיָּבֹא אַרְבֶּה וְיֶלֶק
וְאֵין מִסְפָּר: לה וַיֹּאכַל כָּל־עֵשֶׂב בְּאַרְצָם וַיֹּאכַל פְּרִי אַדְמָתָם: לו וַיַּךְ
כָּל־בְּכוֹר בְּאַרְצָם רֵאשִׁית לְכָל־אוֹנָם: לז וַיּוֹצִיאֵם בְּכֶסֶף וְזָהָב וְאֵין
בִּשְׁבָטָיו כּוֹשֵׁל: לח שָׂמַח מִצְרַיִם בְּצֵאתָם כִּי־נָפַל פַּחְדָּם עֲלֵיהֶם:
לט פָּרַשׂ עָנָן לְמָסָךְ וְאֵשׁ לְהָאִיר לָיְלָה: מ שָׁאַל וַיָּבֵא שְׂלָו [שְׂלָיו]
וְלֶחֶם שָׁמַיִם יַשְׂבִּיעֵם: מא פָּתַח צוּר וַיָּזוּבוּ מָיִם הָלְכוּ בַּצִּיּוֹת נָהָר:
מב כִּי־זָכַר אֶת־דְּבַר קָדְשׁוֹ אֶת־אַבְרָהָם עַבְדּוֹ: מג וַיּוֹצִא עַמּוֹ בְשָׂשׂוֹן
בְּרִנָּה אֶת־בְּחִירָיו: מד וַיִּתֵּן לָהֶם אַרְצוֹת גּוֹיִם וַעֲמַל לְאֻמִּים יִירָשׁוּ:
מה בַּעֲבוּר | יִשְׁמְרוּ חֻקָּיו וְתוֹרֹתָיו יִנְצֹרוּ הַלְלוּיָהּ:

49

* TIKKUN VII *

פרק צ

א תְּפִלָּה לְמֹשֶׁה אִישׁ־הָאֱלֹהִים אֲדֹנָי מָעוֹן אַתָּה הָיִיתָ לָּנוּ בְּדֹר וָדֹר: ב בְּטֶרֶם | הָרִים יֻלָּדוּ וַתְּחוֹלֵל אֶרֶץ וְתֵבֵל וּמֵעוֹלָם עַד־עוֹלָם אַתָּה אֵל: ג תָּשֵׁב אֱנוֹשׁ עַד־דַּכָּא וַתֹּאמֶר שׁוּבוּ בְנֵי־אָדָם: ד כִּי אֶלֶף שָׁנִים בְּעֵינֶיךָ כְּיוֹם אֶתְמוֹל כִּי יַעֲבֹר וְאַשְׁמוּרָה בַלָּיְלָה: ה זְרַמְתָּם שֵׁנָה יִהְיוּ בַּבֹּקֶר כֶּחָצִיר יַחֲלֹף: ו בַּבֹּקֶר יָצִיץ וְחָלָף לָעֶרֶב יְמוֹלֵל וְיָבֵשׁ: ז כִּי־כָלִינוּ בְאַפֶּךָ וּבַחֲמָתְךָ נִבְהָלְנוּ: ח שַׁתָּ [שַׁתָּה] עֲוֹנֹתֵינוּ לְנֶגְדֶּךָ עֲלֻמֵנוּ לִמְאוֹר פָּנֶיךָ: ט כִּי כָל־יָמֵינוּ פָּנוּ בְעֶבְרָתֶךָ כִּלִּינוּ שָׁנֵינוּ כְמוֹ־הֶגֶה: י יְמֵי שְׁנוֹתֵינוּ | בָּהֶם שִׁבְעִים שָׁנָה וְאִם בִּגְבוּרֹת | שְׁמוֹנִים שָׁנָה וְרָהְבָּם עָמָל וָאָוֶן כִּי־גָז חִישׁ וַנָּעֻפָה: יא מִי־יוֹדֵעַ עֹז אַפֶּךָ וּכְיִרְאָתְךָ עֶבְרָתֶךָ: יב לִמְנוֹת יָמֵינוּ כֵּן הוֹדַע וְנָבִא לְבַב חָכְמָה: יג שׁוּבָה יְהוָה עַד־מָתָי וְהִנָּחֵם עַל־עֲבָדֶיךָ: יד שַׂבְּעֵנוּ בַבֹּקֶר חַסְדֶּךָ וּנְרַנְּנָה וְנִשְׂמְחָה בְּכָל־יָמֵינוּ: טו שַׂמְּחֵנוּ כִּימוֹת עִנִּיתָנוּ שְׁנוֹת רָאִינוּ רָעָה: טז יֵרָאֶה אֶל־עֲבָדֶיךָ פָעֳלֶךָ וַהֲדָרְךָ עַל־בְּנֵיהֶם: יז וִיהִי | נֹעַם אֲדֹנָי אֱלֹהֵינוּ עָלֵינוּ וּמַעֲשֵׂה יָדֵינוּ כּוֹנְנָה עָלֵינוּ וּמַעֲשֵׂה יָדֵינוּ כּוֹנְנֵהוּ:

* TIKKUN VI *

פרק עז

א לַמְנַצֵּחַ עַל־יְדִיתוּן [יְדוּתוּן] לְאָסָף מִזְמוֹר: ב קוֹלִי אֶל־אֱלֹהִים וְאֶצְעָקָה קוֹלִי אֶל־אֱלֹהִים וְהַאֲזִין אֵלָי: ג בְּיוֹם צָרָתִי אֲדֹנָי דָּרָשְׁתִּי יָדִי | לַיְלָה נִגְּרָה וְלֹא תָפוּג מֵאֲנָה הִנָּחֵם נַפְשִׁי: ד אַזְכְּרָה אֱלֹהִים וְאֶהֱמָיָה אָשִׂיחָה | וְתִתְעַטֵּף רוּחִי סֶלָה: ה אָחַזְתָּ שְׁמֻרוֹת עֵינָי נִפְעַמְתִּי וְלֹא אֲדַבֵּר: ו חִשַּׁבְתִּי יָמִים מִקֶּדֶם שְׁנוֹת עוֹלָמִים: ז אַזְכְּרָה נְגִינָתִי בַּלָּיְלָה עִם־לְבָבִי אָשִׂיחָה וַיְחַפֵּשׂ רוּחִי: ח הַלְעוֹלָמִים יִזְנַח | אֲדֹנָי וְלֹא־יֹסִיף לִרְצוֹת עוֹד: ט הֶאָפֵס לָנֶצַח חַסְדּוֹ גָּמַר אֹמֶר לְדֹר וָדֹר: י הֲשָׁכַח חַנּוֹת אֵל אִם־קָפַץ בְּאַף רַחֲמָיו סֶלָה: יא וָאֹמַר חַלּוֹתִי הִיא שְׁנוֹת יְמִין עֶלְיוֹן: יב אַזְכִּיר [אֶזְכּוֹר] מַעַלְלֵי־יָהּ כִּי־אַזְכְּרָה מִקֶּדֶם פִּלְאֶךָ: יג וְהָגִיתִי בְכָל־פָּעֳלֶךָ וּבַעֲלִילוֹתֶיךָ אָשִׂיחָה: יד אֱלֹהִים בַּקֹּדֶשׁ דַּרְכֶּךָ מִי־אֵל גָּדוֹל כֵּאלֹהִים: טו אַתָּה הָאֵל עֹשֵׂה פֶלֶא הוֹדַעְתָּ בָעַמִּים עֻזֶּךָ: טז גָּאַלְתָּ בִּזְרוֹעַ עַמֶּךָ בְּנֵי־יַעֲקֹב וְיוֹסֵף סֶלָה | יז רָאוּךָ מַּיִם אֱלֹהִים רָאוּךָ מַּיִם יָחִילוּ אַף יִרְגְּזוּ תְהֹמוֹת: יח זֹרְמוּ מַיִם | עָבוֹת קוֹל נָתְנוּ שְׁחָקִים אַף־חֲצָצֶיךָ יִתְהַלָּכוּ: יט קוֹל רַעַמְךָ | בַּגַּלְגַּל הֵאִירוּ בְרָקִים תֵּבֵל רָגְזָה וַתִּרְעַשׁ הָאָרֶץ: כ בַּיָּם דַּרְכֶּךָ וּשְׁבִילֶיךָ [וּשְׁבִילְךָ] בְּמַיִם רַבִּים וְעִקְּבוֹתֶיךָ לֹא נֹדָעוּ: כא נָחִיתָ כַצֹּאן עַמֶּךָ בְּיַד־מֹשֶׁה וְאַהֲרֹן:

* TIKKUN V *

פרק נט

א לַמְנַצֵּחַ אַל־תַּשְׁחֵת לְדָוִד מִכְתָּם בִּשְׁלֹחַ שָׁאוּל וַיִּשְׁמְרוּ
אֶת־הַבַּיִת לַהֲמִיתוֹ: ב הַצִּילֵנִי מֵאֹיְבַי | אֱלֹהָי מִמִּתְקוֹמְמַי
תְּשַׂגְּבֵנִי: ג הַצִּילֵנִי מִפֹּעֲלֵי אָוֶן וּמֵאַנְשֵׁי דָמִים הוֹשִׁיעֵנִי: ד כִּי
הִנֵּה אָרְבוּ לְנַפְשִׁי יָגוּרוּ עָלַי עַזִּים לֹא־פִשְׁעִי וְלֹא־חַטָּאתִי
יְהֹוָה: ה בְּלִי־עָוֹן יְרֻצוּן וְיִכּוֹנָנוּ עוּרָה לִקְרָאתִי וּרְאֵה:
ו וְאַתָּה יְהֹוָה־אֱלֹהִים | צְבָאוֹת אֱלֹהֵי יִשְׂרָאֵל הָקִיצָה לִפְקֹד
כָּל־הַגּוֹיִם אַל־תָּחֹן כָּל־בֹּגְדֵי אָוֶן סֶלָה: ז יָשׁוּבוּ לָעֶרֶב יֶהֱמוּ
כַכָּלֶב וִיסוֹבְבוּ עִיר: ח הִנֵּה | יַבִּיעוּן בְּפִיהֶם חֲרָבוֹת
בְּשִׂפְתוֹתֵיהֶם כִּי־מִי שֹׁמֵעַ: ט וְאַתָּה יְהֹוָה תִּשְׂחַק־לָמוֹ תִּלְעַג
לְכָל־גּוֹיִם: י עֻזּוֹ אֵלֶיךָ אֶשְׁמֹרָה כִּי־אֱלֹהִים מִשְׂגַּבִּי: יא אֱלֹהֵי
חַסְדּוֹ [חַסְדִּי] יְקַדְּמֵנִי אֱלֹהִים יַרְאֵנִי בְשֹׁרְרָי: יב אַל־תַּהַרְגֵם
| פֶּן־יִשְׁכְּחוּ עַמִּי הֲנִיעֵמוֹ בְחֵילְךָ וְהוֹרִידֵמוֹ מָגִנֵּנוּ אֲדֹנָי:
יג חַטַּאת פִּימוֹ דְּבַר־שְׂפָתֵימוֹ וְיִלָּכְדוּ בִגְאוֹנָם וּמֵאָלָה
וּמִכַּחַשׁ יְסַפֵּרוּ: יד כַּלֵּה בְחֵמָה כַּלֵּה וְאֵינֵמוֹ וְיֵדְעוּ כִּי־אֱלֹהִים
מֹשֵׁל בְּיַעֲקֹב לְאַפְסֵי הָאָרֶץ סֶלָה: טו וְיָשֻׁבוּ לָעֶרֶב יֶהֱמוּ
כַכָּלֶב וִיסוֹבְבוּ עִיר: טז הֵמָּה יְנִיעוּן [יְנוּעוּן] לֶאֱכֹל אִם־לֹא
יִשְׂבְּעוּ וַיָּלִינוּ: יז וַאֲנִי | אָשִׁיר עֻזֶּךָ וַאֲרַנֵּן לַבֹּקֶר חַסְדֶּךָ
כִּי־הָיִיתָ מִשְׂגָּב לִי וּמָנוֹס בְּיוֹם צַר־לִי: יח עֻזִּי אֵלֶיךָ אֲזַמֵּרָה
כִּי־אֱלֹהִים מִשְׂגַּבִּי אֱלֹהֵי חַסְדִּי:

52

* TIKKUN IV *

פרק מב

א לַמְנַצֵּחַ מַשְׂכִּיל לִבְנֵי־קֹרַח: ב כְּאַיָּל תַּעֲרֹג עַל־אֲפִיקֵי־מָיִם כֵּן נַפְשִׁי תַעֲרֹג אֵלֶיךָ אֱלֹהִים: ג צָמְאָה נַפְשִׁי | לֵאלֹהִים לְאֵל חָי מָתַי אָבוֹא וְאֵרָאֶה פְּנֵי אֱלֹהִים: ד הָיְתָה־לִּי דִמְעָתִי לֶחֶם יוֹמָם וָלַיְלָה בֶּאֱמֹר אֵלַי כָּל־הַיּוֹם אַיֵּה אֱלֹהֶיךָ: ה אֵלֶּה אֶזְכְּרָה | וְאֶשְׁפְּכָה עָלַי | נַפְשִׁי כִּי אֶעֱבֹר | בַּסָּךְ אֶדַּדֵּם עַד־בֵּית אֱלֹהִים בְּקוֹל־רִנָּה וְתוֹדָה הָמוֹן חוֹגֵג: ו מַה־תִּשְׁתּוֹחֲחִי | נַפְשִׁי וַתֶּהֱמִי עָלָי הוֹחִילִי לֵאלֹהִים כִּי־עוֹד אוֹדֶנּוּ יְשׁוּעוֹת פָּנָיו: ז אֱלֹהַי עָלַי נַפְשִׁי תִשְׁתּוֹחָח עַל־כֵּן אֶזְכָּרְךָ מֵאֶרֶץ יַרְדֵּן וְחֶרְמוֹנִים מֵהַר מִצְעָר: ח תְּהוֹם אֶל־תְּהוֹם קוֹרֵא לְקוֹל צִנּוֹרֶיךָ כָּל־מִשְׁבָּרֶיךָ וְגַלֶּיךָ עָלַי עָבָרוּ: ט יוֹמָם | יְצַוֶּה יְהוָה | חַסְדּוֹ וּבַלַּיְלָה שִׁירֹה [שִׁירוֹ] עִמִּי תְּפִלָּה לְאֵל חַיָּי: י אוֹמְרָה | לְאֵל סַלְעִי לָמָה שְׁכַחְתָּנִי לָמָּה־קֹדֵר אֵלֵךְ בְּלַחַץ אוֹיֵב: יא בְּרֶצַח | בְּעַצְמוֹתַי חֵרְפוּנִי צוֹרְרָי בְּאָמְרָם אֵלַי כָּל־הַיּוֹם אַיֵּה אֱלֹהֶיךָ: יב מַה־תִּשְׁתּוֹחֲחִי | נַפְשִׁי וּמַה־תֶּהֱמִי עָלָי הוֹחִילִי לֵאלֹהִים כִּי־עוֹד אוֹדֶנּוּ יְשׁוּעֹת פָּנַי וֵאלֹהָי:

* TIKKUN III *

פרק מא

א לַמְנַצֵּחַ מִזְמוֹר לְדָוִד: ב אַשְׁרֵי מַשְׂכִּיל אֶל־דָּל בְּיוֹם רָעָה יְמַלְּטֵהוּ יְהֹוָה: ג יְהֹוָה | יִשְׁמְרֵהוּ וִיחַיֵּהוּ יְאַשַּׁר [וְאֻשַּׁר] בָּאָרֶץ וְאַל־תִּתְּנֵהוּ בְּנֶפֶשׁ אֹיְבָיו: ד יְהֹוָה יִסְעָדֶנּוּ עַל־עֶרֶשׂ דְּוָי כָּל־מִשְׁכָּבוֹ הָפַכְתָּ בְחָלְיוֹ: ה אֲנִי־אָמַרְתִּי יְהֹוָה חָנֵּנִי רְפָאָה נַפְשִׁי כִּי־חָטָאתִי לָךְ: ו אוֹיְבַי יֹאמְרוּ רַע לִי מָתַי יָמוּת וְאָבַד שְׁמוֹ: ז וְאִם־בָּא לִרְאוֹת | שָׁוְא יְדַבֵּר לִבּוֹ יִקְבָּץ־אָוֶן לוֹ יֵצֵא לַחוּץ יְדַבֵּר: ח יַחַד עָלַי יִתְלַחֲשׁוּ כָּל־שֹׂנְאָי עָלַי | יַחְשְׁבוּ רָעָה לִי: ט דְּבַר־בְּלִיַּעַל יָצוּק בּוֹ וַאֲשֶׁר שָׁכַב לֹא־יוֹסִיף לָקוּם: י גַּם אִישׁ־שְׁלוֹמִי | אֲשֶׁר־בָּטַחְתִּי בוֹ אוֹכֵל לַחְמִי הִגְדִּיל עָלַי עָקֵב: יא וְאַתָּה יְהֹוָה חָנֵּנִי וַהֲקִימֵנִי וַאֲשַׁלְּמָה לָהֶם: יב בְּזֹאת יָדַעְתִּי כִּי־חָפַצְתָּ בִּי כִּי לֹא־יָרִיעַ אֹיְבִי עָלָי: יג וַאֲנִי בְּתֻמִּי תָּמַכְתָּ בִּי וַתַּצִּיבֵנִי לְפָנֶיךָ לְעוֹלָם | יד בָּרוּךְ יְהֹוָה | אֱלֹהֵי יִשְׂרָאֵל מֵהָעוֹלָם וְעַד הָעוֹלָם אָמֵן | וְאָמֵן:

* TIKKUN II *

פרק לב

א לְדָוִד מַשְׂכִּיל אַשְׁרֵי נְשׂוּי־פֶּשַׁע כְּסוּי חֲטָאָה: ב אַשְׁרֵי־אָדָם לֹא יַחְשֹׁב יְהֹוָה לוֹ עָוֹן וְאֵין בְּרוּחוֹ רְמִיָּה: ג כִּי־הֶחֱרַשְׁתִּי בָּלוּ עֲצָמָי בְּשַׁאֲגָתִי כָּל־הַיּוֹם: ד כִּי | יוֹמָם וָלַיְלָה | תִּכְבַּד עָלַי יָדֶךָ נֶהְפַּךְ לְשַׁדִּי בְּחַרְבֹנֵי קַיִץ סֶלָה: ה חַטָּאתִי אוֹדִיעֲךָ וַעֲוֹנִי לֹא־כִסִּיתִי אָמַרְתִּי אוֹדֶה עֲלֵי פְשָׁעַי לַיהֹוָה וְאַתָּה נָשָׂאתָ עֲוֹן חַטָּאתִי סֶלָה: ו עַל־זֹאת יִתְפַּלֵּל כָּל־חָסִיד | אֵלֶיךָ לְעֵת מְצֹא רַק לְשֵׁטֶף מַיִם רַבִּים אֵלָיו לֹא יַגִּיעוּ: ז אַתָּה | סֵתֶר לִי מִצַּר תִּצְּרֵנִי רָנֵּי פַלֵּט תְּסוֹבְבֵנִי סֶלָה: ח אַשְׂכִּילְךָ | וְאוֹרְךָ בְּדֶרֶךְ־זוּ תֵלֵךְ אִיעֲצָה עָלֶיךָ עֵינִי: ט אַל־תִּהְיוּ | כְּסוּס כְּפֶרֶד אֵין הָבִין בְּמֶתֶג וָרֶסֶן עֶדְיוֹ לִבְלוֹם בַּל קְרֹב אֵלֶיךָ: י רַבִּים מַכְאוֹבִים לָרָשָׁע וְהַבּוֹטֵחַ בַּיהֹוָה חֶסֶד יְסוֹבְבֶנּוּ: יא שִׂמְחוּ בַיהֹוָה וְגִילוּ צַדִּיקִים וְהַרְנִינוּ כָּל־יִשְׁרֵי־לֵב:

* TIKKUN I *

פרק טז

א מִכְתָּם לְדָוִד שָׁמְרֵנִי אֵל כִּי־חָסִיתִי בָךְ: ב אָמַרְתְּ לַיהוָה אֲדֹנָי אָתָּה טוֹבָתִי בַּל־עָלֶיךָ: ג לִקְדוֹשִׁים אֲשֶׁר־בָּאָרֶץ הֵמָּה וְאַדִּירֵי כָּל־חֶפְצִי־בָם: ד יִרְבּוּ עַצְּבוֹתָם אַחֵר מָהָרוּ בַּל־אַסִּיךְ נִסְכֵּיהֶם מִדָּם וּבַל־אֶשָּׂא אֶת־שְׁמוֹתָם עַל־שְׂפָתָי: ה יְהוָה מְנָת־חֶלְקִי וְכוֹסִי אַתָּה תּוֹמִיךְ גּוֹרָלִי: ו חֲבָלִים נָפְלוּ־לִי בַּנְּעִמִים אַף־נַחֲלָת שָׁפְרָה עָלָי: ז אֲבָרֵךְ אֶת־יְהוָה אֲשֶׁר יְעָצָנִי אַף־לֵילוֹת יִסְּרוּנִי כִלְיוֹתָי: ח שִׁוִּיתִי יְהוָה לְנֶגְדִּי תָמִיד כִּי מִימִינִי בַּל־אֶמּוֹט: ט לָכֵן | שָׂמַח לִבִּי וַיָּגֶל כְּבוֹדִי אַף־בְּשָׂרִי יִשְׁכֹּן לָבֶטַח: י כִּי | לֹא־תַעֲזֹב נַפְשִׁי לִשְׁאוֹל לֹא־תִתֵּן חֲסִידְךָ לִרְאוֹת שָׁחַת: יא תּוֹדִיעֵנִי אֹרַח חַיִּים שֹׂבַע שְׂמָחוֹת אֶת־פָּנֶיךָ נְעִמוֹת בִּימִינְךָ נֶצַח:

56

Printed in Great Britain
by Amazon

86524159R00041